The Limerickiad

The Limerickiad:
Volume IV

from Tolstoy
to Modernism

Martin Rowson

Smoke STACK BOOKS

Smokestack Books
1 Lake Terrace, Grewelthorpe, Ripon HG4 3BU
e-mail: info@smokestack-books.co.uk
www.smokestack-books.co.uk

ISBN 978-0-9934547-7-6

Smokestack Books is represented by Inpress Ltd

Thanks are due to the *Independent on Sunday*, where some of these poems first appeared.

Dedication

For the record, it takes DEDICATION
To pen stuff for your delectation
   Knowing some blogger'll
   Denounce it as doggerel
Saying I need medication!

Still, I DEDICATE this book to those
To whom the poor feeble thing owes
   Its life. Therefore hand the
   Garlands to ANDY
Plus – always – FRED, ANNA and ROSE

Contents

Tsarist Russia

This will come as a terrible wrench,
But we're in a NEW VOLUME. The French
    And their decadent ways
    Now repel, and our gaze
Flits to other Lits, well worth a mensh,

Where princes' lives couldn't get plusher
Though a glance from the door of the dacha*
    Shows the steppe with slush sodden
    And the peasants downtrodden,
So welcome, folks, to TSARIST RUSSIA!

The Lit responded, on the whole,
By showing the peasantry's role
    Was to suffer despair
    And then die, cos they're there
To plump up a novelist's soul.

While novels take a-away your breath see
The Tsar's censors rant! 'Damn that pesky
    TURGENEV! Oy oy!
    He's worse than TOLSTOY
Let alone that creep F DOSTOYEVSKY!'

---

*   This rhyme makes me look like a pillock
    Transliterated from Cyrillic**

** And while we're about it – oh hell!
    I suppose that this rhyme does as well...

Gogol and Turgenev

The great Russian writer GOGOL's
Looked at his homeland's podsols*,
    That rich Russian earth,
    And responded with mirth!
It's there in his novel *DEAD SOULS*

Where the hero's a trickster whose hoax
On petty officialdom pokes
    Fun amidst laughter
    Though writers hereafter
Often will leave out the jokes.

Take TURGENEV's *FATHERS AND SONS*
Where it seems almost all of the fun's
    Concerned with the schism
    Between Nihilism
And Liberals. Plus, there's no puns**

And though, to be honest, I'm glad
No one sobs, 'Love you son!' 'Love you dad!',
    When dissecting society
    With such heightened piety
Would a few gags be that retrograd?

*   I can see from your face you abhor
    This rhyme. It's translation once more.

** I know no critic who can pull off
    A joke in the name 'Barazov'...

Leo Tolstoy

We now come to LEO TOLSTOY
Who found many ways to annoy
    The Orthodox Church
    Whom he would besmirch
For their Christian shortcomings! Oy!

Their worldliness, he would insist
With an agonised flick of the wrist,
    Made them hubristical.
    'Be far more mystical
And live like Our Lord!' That's the gist.

For you can o'ercome limitation
By living without complication:
    'Till the land! Cut the turf!
    Love your God! Love your serf!
Then die in a provincial station!'*

To this end Tolstoy toiled without cease.
To coax his soul's final release
    Through service to God
    Though frankly the sod
Is bestest know for *WAR AND PEACE.*

* An end for which all truly yearn
  And yet... should one buy a return?

War and Peace

At a soiree PRINCE ANDREI and PIERRE
In their own different fashions prepare
    For War! ANDREI's posh
    While the ROSTOVS seem gauche*
And DOLOKHOV's bad, so beware!

If you'd like to know the true costov
Land Management, don't ask a ROSTOV.
    Pierre duels**. Austerlitz
    Sees Andrei blown to bits
And that's Book 2 more or less tossedov.

Dumped by NATASHA, ANDREI's jaded.
PIERRE's idealism has faded
    Though now the book's more
    Or less about War
Because BONAPARTE has invaded.

NAPOLEON retreats with PIERRE.
ANDREI dies of his wounds, beyond care,
    First forgiving NATASH
    And so – bish bosh bash! –
She now marries PIERRE! The End! Yeah!

Epilogue
Some survive. Others take early baths,
And TOLSTOY says History's like Maths…

---

*   In translation this doesn't quite rhyme,
    But this book's bloody thick! Give it time!

** Does it matter that PIERRE's embracin'
    The sinister life of the Mason?

Anna Karenina

High born Russian women and men in a
Frenzy of lust should think 'When in a
    Hole, best stop digging.'
    Instead all these frigging
Russkies, like ANNA KARENINA

And VRONSKY and KITTY, like ten in a
Bed romps with LEVIN (not LENIN, a
    Bolshevik – reds
    Prefer sex under beds).
Private Dicks paid hard cash to be pennin' a

Report on this filth quake and then in a
Trice drop dead! Dogs in a den in a
    Ditch don't behave as
    Bad as these ravers
It's too much for ANNA KARENINA

Who jumps 'neath a train! Don't repine,
Cos LEVIN finds Jesus! Well, fine.
    But for other folk, who knew
    Their late train was due to
Fallen lovers on the line?

Tolstoy's other Fiction

Among *THE COSSACKS* one called LUKA
Is shot when he tries to rebuke a
    Chechen! MARYANKA,
    His bird, cries 'You wanker!'
When posh DIMITRIY tries to fuka.

Cossacks, by and large, tend to pillage
At random each next peasant village
    Though they are not to blame
    Midst the terror and shame
For *THE DEATH OF IVAN ILYICH*.

Whether Russian or Cossack or Tartar,
All love is foul, just for a starter,
    And as vile as all life!
    Why not murder your wife
And walk free? That's *THE KREUTZER SONATA*.

Tolstoy's last book's called *RESURRECTION*
In which he concludes, on reflection,
    That God's love has a hitch:
    Human life's *still* a bitch!
Took his time working out that connection...

Dostoyevsky

Whereas Football has Emile Heskey
And Ice Hockey boasts Wayne Gretzky
    If you want RUSSIAN LIT's
    Hottest hot hits
Then peruse the works of DOSTOYEVSKY!

As pungent as 12 year old whesky
He could make the blind hear and the deaf see*
    Though you'll find on the whole,
    Deep in that Russian soul,
It gets rather grim. 'DOSTOYEVSKY!'

His editors cried, 'why this pesky
Endless lamentable death spree?!
    This stuff's worse than Mordor!
    We want more joke, Fyodor!'
'Life is meaningless,' moaned DOSTOYEVSKY.

So if you are trolling down Nevsky
Prospekt high on crystal meth, see?
    You'd be wrong to assume
    You're escaping the gloom
That pervades the oeuvre of DOSTOYEVSKY...

* I concede, as this sounds unprofound
  I may have got this wrong way round.

Crime and Punishment

RASKALNIKOV isn't a nutter.
He just seems like one, given his utter
    Contempt for all morals
    Which makes him pick quarrels
With nasty old women. (We mutter

At this point, does this whole thing feel
As if any of it could be real?
    But to hell with the facts!)
    So. R wielded an axe
To kill two old dears! How they squeal!

He'd get away with it, apart
From SONYA, a kind-hearted tart,
    To whom he confesses
    Confirming the guesses
Of PORFIRY*, who'd sussed from the start.

That's the CRIME dealt with. Now for the PUNISHMENT –
Though this might cause general astunishment:
    You'd think he's get banged
    Up in chokey, or hanged...
He gets just 8 years internal bunishment!!**

---

*   He's the cop. You don't need SHERLOCK HOLMES
    When you've seen how RASKALNIKOV foams.

** The court might as well simply go
    And give the toerag an Asbo!

The Brothers Karamazov

At the birth of each bro KARAMAZOV
Their family rejoiced and cried 'Hats off!'
    Then many years later
    FYODOR their pater
Had effectively pissed all three brats off!

What lights up a KARAMAZOV?
Lust! God! Doubt! Avarice! Wrath!
    That's DMITRI and IVAN
    While ALOYSHA's off strivin'
With monks and a sick schoolboy's cough.

An old monk dies and starts to go off
While DMITRI's out having a boff!
    Then after a while
    There's a dreadful mistrial
When a *fourth* Brother KARAMAZOV

Chops through old FYODOR's aorta!
With his final breath maybe he thought a
    Much better bet
    To avoid all this sweat
Would've been to've had just one daughter.

The Idiot

PRINCE MYSHKIN is thick and has fits;
His mate ROGOZHIN often hits
    His girls, a propensity
    Of savage intensity.
Don't you love Russians to bits?

The book's plot thereafter gets tangled
As prospects of marriage are dangled
    And then withdrawn quick
    From MYSHKIN (who's thick)
And ROGOZHIN's girlfriend gets mangled.

As a view of life things don't get drearier
Than this, nor the readers much wearier
    So we're secretly glad
    When MYSHKIN goes mad
And ROGOZHIN's sent to Siberia!

Yet when all people want is good cheer
And the book – a bestseller! – was dear
    At 12 roubles a pop
    From your nearest bookshop
Just *who* are the idiots round here?

A Moody Russian
Sole

The European Novel

The mid-19th Century's blessed
With Great Russian Novels, yet west
    Of that rich Russian earth
    There's a huge novel dearth
Til you get far as France. For the rest

Despite the occasional fellah
Like your German boys FREYTAG or KELLER,
    In Mittel-Europa
    A dose of L-DOPA
Won't bring forth a global bestseller!

Why was Central Europe benighted?
Several reasons are cited:
    Hapsburg Empire's a wreck;
    No one yet writes in CZECH;
Germany isn't united.

And South of the Alps, if you went to
Milan via Rome and Sorento,
    'There's no LIT in ITALY,'
    The locals cried bitterly.
'We're having a RISORGIMENTO!'

Hans Christian Andersen

Central Europe mid-century's weak
On LIT, though if you fancy bleak
    Yet powerful LIT
    Simply go North a bit
And there you will find what you seek!

Beyond Schleswig-Holstein the Danes
Were making phenomenal gains!
    Philosophy's hard
    But they had KIERKEGAARD
While HANS CHRISTIAN ANDERSEN's brains

Poured forth Fairy Tales so torrential
They're still globally influential:
    Little Mermaids! Fir Trees!
    Swans! Princesses and Peas!
While KIERKEGAARD got existential!

This creative ferment was thrilling,
But also decidedly chilling:
    Mermaids turned into spray;
    The tree gets burnt; but hey!
If you want light relief watch *THE KILLING*!

Ibsen

You want Nordic Noir of a blacker black?
Then shift your arse over the Skagerrak
    And head up North West
    Where you'll find you've been blessed
With a Lit that's akin to a frack attack.

I sing now of Lit that Norwegian,
Of that Lit which is endlessly squeegin'
    Such pain out of Norway
    The theatre doorway
Is jammed as they flee by the legion.

Cos it's dark half the year, and the souls
Of the folk, when not harried by trolls,
    Were scoured! They'd cry 'Gawd!
    Not another fjord!?'
As they'd eat pickled seals from tin bowls.

Does the location give us a hint
Of Norwegian writing's blueprint?
    As collected by MOE*
    Their dark folk tales show
The way straight to IBSEN's *PEER GYNT*...

* ORGEN MOE was the finest of men
  Like his colleague and pal ASBJORNSEN.

Peer Gynt

He's selfish and weak, is PEER GYNT,
And his dad's left the family skint!
    At his bird's wedding feast
    PEER gets pissed as a beast
And then runs away with the bint!

For kidnapping the bride, bad PEER GYNT
Is banished so goes for a stint
    Of long mountain strolls
    Where he falls in with trolls
And a thing called a 'Boyg'.* By dint

Of his dithering ego PEER GYNT
Never gets round to taking the hint
    Til he's ravaged by fear!
    Death trolls off with poor PEER
As cool as an after-eight mint**.

As a drama *PEER GYNTs'* in a league
Of its own: symbolism; intrigue;
    The way it gets trollier...
    But it's all rendered jollier
By the music composed by E GRIEG!

---

*   With its troll maidens, this play won't spoil
    If you say it's just 'Boyg meets Gargoyle'.

** Though you hope that's the last of the dope
    The play ends with a glimmer of hope.

Brand

There once was the priest name of BRAND
Who tried to make folk understand
    You must live your life fully!
    But BRAND was a bully:
Things didn't turn out as he'd planned.

With his best friend's girlfriend, hand in hand,
They have a son whose health can't stand
    Their glacial home
    From which BRAND won't roam
So the kid croaks. There's no magic wand*

To make things get better for BRAND.
He won't grieve, though he heeds the demand
    For his dead son's old raiments.
    For this act his payment's
His wife died too! Strike up the band!

BRAND's congregation, having planned
To love him, drive BRAND off their land.
    BRAND's alone. We all blanche.
    Then a huge avalanche
Comes to finish him off! Ain't life grand?

* This rhyme works in that far off region
  Where everyone speaks in Norwegian.

A Doll's House

There once was this woman called NORA
Who lived in the land where Aurora
    Borealis shine bright,
    And yet NORA's life's shite
Cos she once forged a loan. Did PANDORA

Release woes as legion as NORA?
Loan helped hubby's health. He's a bore, a
    Prig, but this clerk'll
    Get all Patriarchal!
Yet NORA adored him. Oh, sure, a

Mum's suicide might restore a
Happy home, but there's still more o'
    This blackmail and crap
    While DOC. RANK's got the clap
Thanks to sins like they had in Gomorrah!

NORA's rumbled. Hubby: 'I deplore a
Lying wife!' Knock at the door. A
    Letter! All's well!
    She's forgiven? Like hell.
'I'm outa this doll's house!' cries NORA.

MORAL:
Don't treat women like toys or old biddies
Or they'll leave leaving you with the kiddies.

Ghosts

In Ibsen's *GENGANGERE* or *GHOSTS*
Widowed Mrs H ALVING toasts
    Her late husband's shade
    With an orphanage paid
For with his fortune. She hosts

Her spiritual guide, who's a Pastor
Who's told the dead spouse was a bastar-
    D who, with remorse,
    She couldn't divorce
Cos her community would then blast her.

Plus her son OSWALD, thanks to dead Mister
ALVING has many a blister
    From congenital syph'lis
    And moreover, with this*
It turns out his girlfriend's his sister.

So all women suffer, while chaps
Are degenerates. OZ has a relapse:
    'The sun,' he moans. 'Suuuun!'
    Bless us all, everyone!
And with luck now the audience claps.

* If this tortuous rhyme doesn't please
  Try having a social disease.

SCANDI—LIT

An Enemy of the People

There once was a doctor called STOCKMANN
Told his brother, the Mayor, 'this may shock. Ban
    The baths we've just built
    Cos they're up to the hilt
With the tannery's waste!' 'You talk cock, man!

Those baths bring us gold in a crock! Can
You please fill your mouth with a sock?' ran
    His brother's reply.
    Doc STOCKMANN thought 'I'
M twixt a hard place and a rock!' An

Answer's to tug his forelock an'
Bend to the will of the flock. Can
    The Majority be WRONG???
    You bet! And they pong!*
Concludes People's Enemy STOCKMANN.

* STOCKMANN isn't having a laugh:
  These bastards all need a good bath.

SCANDI-LIT (cont.)

The Wild Duck

The characters in *THE WILD DUCK*
Should've realised that Ibsen's a schmuck.
    He'll spin morals and lies
    And before the kid dies
They might work that they've run out of luck.*

* Is this too little on *THE WILD DUCK*?
  By this stage I don't give a fuck.

Hedda Gabler

There once was this chick HEDDA GABLER
Whose husband GEORGE was no mere dabbler
    In Academe's Groves.
    Yet selling in droves
Is LOVBORG's book (though *sous le table**

LOVBORG drank himself)! Now rehabler-
Tated, he's no mere drunk babbler
    And his next book will steal
    The professorship they feel
Is GEORGE's. So thinks HEDDA GABLER.

Then GEORGE finds L's Ms., with BRACK,
And HEDDA goes on the attack:
    'Top yourself, L!' cries HEDDA;
    Puts L's book through the shredder!
In a brothel HED's pistol goes 'crack!'**

LOVBORG's dead, and it's messy. But redder
Was HEDDA's face when JUDGE BRACK said her
    Crime was known! BRACK: 'Frail!
    You'll submit to blackmail!'
So she shoots herself. HEDDA's now deader.***

*   This rhyme may give off a foul stench
     But the wine LOVBORG drank was all French.

** HEDDA lent LOVBORG her gun.
     My word, children, isn't this fun?

*** BRACK cries: 'But no one does such things!'
     And it's then that the fat lady sings.

The Master Builder

Having seen the cut of IBSEN's jib
We've sussed that the man's far from glib
    And the Nordic Lifestyle
    Is thus leavened with bile
That exudes, with a spurt, from his nib.

Try this: SOLNESS, the Master Builder
Is beguiled by this young chick called HILDE.
    His wife lives: their children
    Were all beastly killed when*
A house burned down. Doesn't bewilder

SOLNESS. His next building is TAAAALL,
So tall it makes young HILDE drawl:
    'Climb! Sod your vertigo!'
    And so, just to flirt, he go...
We know the poor schmuck's going to fall.

Yet with Nordic Design it is clear
That a true Master Builder would veer
    From Ibsenite gloom
    To a nice bright white room
Scattered with stuff from Ikea!**

* 'Children/killed when' – ah God, this rhyme
  Takes IBSEN beyond the sublime!

** You seek despair? How man has fallen?
   Then seek for that key named by ALLEN!!

SCANDI-LIT (more of it)

Little Eyolf

ALFRED and his missus, named RITA,
Have a nipper called EYOLF who's sweeter
    Than honey from hornets
    Yet since he's been born it's
Been tough. When ALF gave REET a treat (a

Roll in the sack) from the table'd
Rolled EYOLF! Now he's disabled.
    REET's jealous; regretful
    Is ALF – and neglectful.
Family Life ain't all it's been fabled.

And then the Rat-Lady comes round.
'Drahn yer rats in the sea fer a pound!'
    'No!' ALF says. The wimp
    Doesn't spot EYOLF limp
After Rat-Lady. EYOLF gets drowned.*

No inquiry is called or adjourned;
No social workers blamed, then spurned.
    RITA's redemption bid is
    Working with kiddies!!?!
So it seems that no lessons were learned.

* For kiddies in IBSEN their wages
  Is Death. We've all know this for ages.

John Gabriel Borkman

BORKMAN the Banker's done time
For a hideous financial crime.
   'Hoorah!' cries Mankind
   But I think that you'll find
That we all have a mountain to climb.

His wife GUNHILD thinks that his shame's
Blackened their son ERHART's names.
   She invests, with sis ELLA,
   Hope in the young fella
Who instead scarpers South with some dames.

Since nick BORKMAN's lurked for eight years
In his room upstairs, but now appears!
   'I stole,' he's now whining,
   'To invest in some mining!'
They go out to seek fresh nadirs

So JOHN, EL and GUN are now found
Up the Mountain, while deep underground
   Lies metal! JOHN said,
   'We'll be rich!' then dropped dead.
Ain't it great to see life in the round?

When We Dead Awaken

Thank God! Unless I'm much mistaken
We've reached IBSEN's last play! I'm makin'
    Assumptions he'll stick
    With his usual shtik
Of Death, Gloom and Lives Godforsaken.

But I could be wrong. Maybe he's taken
A spy who drinks – not stirred, but shaken –
    Strong stuff from a glass;
    Or written a farce
That features a comedy Kraken,*

Or some Chicklit about women fakin'
Their orgasms or – I know! Bakin'!
    His gloom he'd soon shake off
    With The Great IBSEN Bake Off!!!
But no. In *WHEN WE DEAD AWAKEN*

A sculptor called RUBEK's** partaken
Of flirtations, then gets overtaken
    By an avalanche***. Cor.
    We've heard that one before.
When it's finished I might reawaken.

*   In a Maelstrom off Bergen you'll find
    Shoals of sea-beasts of this kind.

** RUBEK's a jerk; he's a roob;
    He's not simply square; RUBEK's *cube*.

*** He first pulled this trick off in *BRAND*
    So we cry one last time: 'ain't life grand?'

Strindberg

IBSEN's been done in good order
So let us troll over the border
    To Sweden (that's East).
    Here STRINDBERG released
Yet more drama with gloom underscored. A

Strange man, his life was unruly;
Obsessed with the occult and truly
    Thinking Realism's best
    His marbles went west
But first STRINDBERG knocked out *MISS JULIE*.

The plot: JULIE's dad is a count
Although she's up for any amount
    Of low-lifes and rough
    Til dancing ain't enough.
Like with JEAN the valet, who's a fount

Of flirting and come-ons: he'll praise her;
They'll run off; run an inn; then he lays her.
    Then her dad's home. No prizes
    To guess what arises.
She then tops herself with a razor.*

* I'm also refusing all bets
  On the fates that befall JULIE's pets:
  Bird's beheaded! Dog has an abortion!
  That STRINDBERG, eh? My, what a caution.

An Interruption

At which point we reach a lacuna
That maybe we should have reached sooner.
   For to be very blunt
   Some cilistine phunt
(In the words of the REVEREND SPOONER)

Tried to kill off this epic right here!
This stuff, you see, did first appear
   In a paper each Sunday*
   Though I'm guessing by Monday
They'd line budgies' cages. Don't sneer,

For though witless critics attacked me
FORWARD BOOK OF POETRY backed me!
   Published one! Joy complete!
   My poetic conceit
Meant the paper immediately sacked me

Only two-thirds through this panorama
Of Lit (novels, poetry, drama)
   Which I will now resume!
   So please dance round the room
And forget all that shit about Karma!

* *THE INDEPENDENT ON SUNDAY* its name.
  It no longer exists. What a shame.

George Eliot

Timewise we're at sixes and sevens
So let's turn back the clock and – Good Heavens!
   It's the way she doth telliot!
   Who's that? Why, GEORGE ELIOT!
The pen-name of MARY ANN EVANS.

A loose-living atheist, she'd
Produced English Lit's greatest read
   In that great Gothic Arch
   Of a book, *MIDDLEMARCH,*
But let's begin with *ADAM BEDE...*

Adam Bede

Honest ADAM would like to pet HETTY,
But the SQUIRE, ART and HETTY get sweaty
   And then HETTY hid
   The subsequent kid
Who dies. Now no chance of confetti

Though H got engaged to A BEDE
After ADAM made posh ARTHUR bleed
   As they fought over HET,
   Although right now I'd bet
For the kiddy's death HET hangs. Agreed?

Her cuz DINAH's a Methodist preacher
And in HETTY's cell tries to reach her
   And squeeze some contrition
   Out of her position
But then ARTHUR turns up, a feature

Of novels. The woman he's banged
As a consequence doesn't get hanged
   But transported, while DINAH
   Develops a shine... er...
For ADAM! And wedding bells clanged.

Silas Marner

SILAS MARNER gets framed for a crime;
Moves away, and then after a time
   Earns more swag which he hoards
   Which gets nicked! This affords
SI to chance on a new paradigm.

A girl aged two knocks on his door:
Her mum's gobbled opium! Before
   They can track her down, oh!
   Mummy's stiff in the snow!
Now co-incidences galore

Emerge. The Squire's family, CASS,
Sired a son who nicked SI's gold; alas
   His older bro's bad
   As well; he's the dad
Of the junkie's small kid! What a gas!

Years pass. SILAS now counts his riches
In the life of the little girl, which is
   Worth far more than gold.
   He grows happy and old
Which is nice, but we're hardly in stitches.

The Mill on the Floss

The folk in *THE MILL ON THE FLOSS*
Are accustomed to heartbreak and loss.
    MAGGIE seeks higher things
    Yet has Romantic flings
Suitably racked with pathos.

Her brother TOM thinks he's the boss
But his brotherly love cannot gloss
    O'er M's hots for PHIL WAKEM*,
    Dad's rival's son! 'Make 'em
Cease!' cries TOM, clearly quite cross.

Years pass. MAG's dad dies. 'Come across
To my place,' Cousin LUCE says. 'Th'ethos
    Is of culture and art!'
    Boyfriend STEPHEN, a fart,
Fancies MAGS and does not give a toss.

They sail off downstream. Some kudos
To MAGS when she dumps him. Chaos
    Ensues; floods come down:
    TOM and MAGGIE both drown!
It's less miserable in Westeros!

THE MEAL ON THE FLOSS

Felix Holt, the Radical

In this novel The Great Reform Act
Is served up as fiction and packed
   With action, when TRANSOME
   Comes back from East, handsome
And standing for Parliament, backed

By Radicals like FELIX HOLT
Who'll soon give proceedings a jolt,
   And insure things get gory:
   TRANSOME's folks are Tory!
He won't win this seat by default.

Both men fancy ESTHER, REV LYON's
Step-daughter, although true scion
   Of some wealthy nob's,
   While T's lawyer robs
The family estate without tryin'.

The election arrives! It ain't quiet:
FELIX kills a cop in a riot!
   The Tory's elected
   And so well connected
He gets FELIX off! I don't buy it.*

* They're nasty but Tories ain't dim:
  So what's in this fix up for him?

Middlemarch

DOROTHEA BROOKE, in *MIDDLEMARCH*
Marries CASAUBON, stiffer than starch,
  Whose scholarship's poor
  Though his cuz, LADISLAW
Shows that Love can, at last, overarch.*

* There's much more to this book, I concede;
  More indeed, than most people can read;
  About doctors who fall into debt;
  Businessmen who break out in a sweat
  When the source of their ill-gotten gains
  Are revealed; then there's also the pains
  Of young gentlemen bound for the Church
  Who, when wills change, are left in the lurch;
  Plus a wealth of stuff I could report
  But life is quite simply too short.

Daniel Deronda

GWENDOLEN couldn't be fonder
Of the eponymous DANIEL DERONDA
   Who redeemed a necklace
   She's pawned. Thus disgrace
Is for a while longer kept yonder.

Things get worse and make GWEN then resort
To marry the ghastly GRANDCOURT
   To keep off the skids,
   Though his mistress and kids
Greet the news with a withering snort.

Meanwhile noble DANIEL DERONDA
Falls for MIRAH, a singer. They ponder
   On how they'll find joy
   Seeing he is a goy
And she's Jewish, destined to wander.

MORDECAI cries 'A Homeland! Believe!'
GRANDCOURT drowns, but GWEN doesn't grieve.
   Brought up thinking he's posher*
   Dan now finds he's kosher!*
Weds MIRAH! Next stop, TEL AVIV!

* If you think this rhyme reads overdid-ish
  Just try is again, but in Yiddish...

A Critical Digression

GEORGE ELIOT's novels enforce
The idea of England's divorce
   Of the Self from the Local,
   Empowering the yokel.
She also had teeth like a horse.

Though Leavisite critics get cross*
To ignore these plain facts is our loss
   And to prove dental care
   Wasn't just her affair
Consider 'The Meal on the Floss'!!!

All right, leave it out! Please don't wallop
This poetaster for that dollop
   Of lighthearted fun!
   With fun we're now done.
Let's move on to the novels of TROLLOPE...

* Who despite their clear reverence for words
  Are now rarer than rocking horse turds.

Anthony Trollope

Every morning just wearing his socks
TROLLOPE wrote, then chased after a fox
    Whilst administ'ring The Post
    In which role he could boast
He invented the red pillar box!*

He wrote of the Church's estate
In ways I'll now seek to truncate:
    Thoughts of Deans' daughters' knickers
    And low plots by vicars
Dominate these books, in sextuplate.

If that's all too mitre-y and chalice-r,
Instead you can read of the PALLISER
    Clan! (Gets quite soapy
    And plotwise just dopey
Does Victorian Lit get much Dallas-er?)

Nonetheless several very well read
Statesman have publicly said
    That these books are so neat
    Nothing else can quite beat
Curling up with a TROLLOPE in bed!**

*   This self-serving ruse shows some brass neck,
    Just to post him his royalty cheque!

** Thus spake PM HAROLD MACMILLAN:
    Unlike PROFUMO he was just chillin'.

The Way We Live Now

With the Church and the State thus harpooned
Trollope turned to High Finance; dragooned
   A cast of grotesques
   Sat behind massive desks.
From toffs loads of swag's importuned

By MELMOTTE, the bent railway tsar
Who came to London from afar
   And becomes an MP
   Then goes bust. Here you see
A neo-liberal exemplar.*

* If this sounds familiar, his Muse
  Must've watched last night's 10 o'clock News!

Lewis Carroll

At this point in Victoria's reign
The Rational is getting a pain.
    Being empirical?
    Wholly inimical
To the shit going on in your brain!

Plus you seldom require a barrel
For chaps dressed in vicars' apparel
    Or Professors of Maths
    When you harvest the laffs
They command – until LEWIS CARROLL.

For his Nonsense was ever so droll.
When ALICE popped down a deep hole
    Pursuing a bunny
    Who's late, it's so funny!
This nonsense still failed to console

Those rational minds who go figure
When Alice is small, then much bigger
    Down a hole, chasing fur
    Drowned in tears and... Oo-er!
You don't need much Freudian rigour

To interpret the dreams of that hussy* –
Brown hatters with hares?!? – as abusey*:
    Stealing tarts; hookahs; red
    Old queens wanting head
And a vanishing wide grinning pussy!!!*

* If you think these rhymes don't do the job
  They're NONSENSE, you gibbering knob!

I concede there'll be some find this reading
Of the ALICE books slightly misleading
    But be honest! They're filth!
    The RED QUEEN's just a MILF!
You know, when the obvious is bleeding,

That this nonsense ain't just poppycocky
But from his sub-conscious, ad-hoc-y,
    As he hunted his snark
    In bed after dark
And snicker-snacked his *JABBERWOCKY*.**

** When Carroll got reely and writhey
   Did his borogoves end up all slithey?

Darwin

But relax! Moralists getting preachy's
Premature; everything's peachy! 'S
    Four decades til FREUD;
    The whole world's still annoyed
By DARWIN's *ORIGIN OF SPECIES*!*

This book argued every last punk, he's
Descended from gibbering monkeys!
    The laity gape
    While the clergy go ape
Along with their various flunkeys.

You doubt the truth of this opinion?
Have you just never noticed the simian
    Waddling gait
    Of your average prelate?
The explanation is Darwinian!

* If these rhymes from your tongue have not rolled
  It's your fault. You're *so* unevolved!

SCIENCE & THE IRRATIONAL IN THE MID-VICTORIAN EPOCH

TH Huxley

The clergy now led the attack
Even though if you go further back
    The Bishop of Chester
    Shared an ancestor*
With a chimpanzee *and* a macaque!

They argued away until weary,
The bishops increasingly teary
    Taunted by TH HUXLEY**
    Who left all in flux! We
Can thank your man C DARWIN's theory.

*   His Grace Bishop of Bath & Wells
    Also shares most of their smells.

** See? DARWIN's truth shines through the fog!
    HUXLEY was 'DARWIN's *bulldog*'
    Priests said 'Man's soul means he's no crittur!'
    But that argument's right down the shitter!

The Oxford Movement

We return to REV L CARROLL leching
Over young ALICE LIDDELL. How fetching!
    And this points, I'm afraid,
    To the role Oxford played
In this age's Lit & Thought, stretching

From the Oxford Movement, for starters.
Here you move from The Broad up past Martyrs
    From your C of E home
    Til you almost reach Rome*
And a lifetime of 'Nomine Paters'

While stuck in that college of Keble's.
Here sat chaps so precious that 'feeble''s
    Hardly the word!
    Had it ever occurred
How their smells and bells might play in Peebles?

* Travelling on your knees you know that if
  You smell incense you've arrived. Sniff.

Cardinal Newman

There was a fine cleric called NEWMAN
Whose Kindly Light led to The True! Man
    Will change, dreams GERONTIUS
    Because God would wantius
To stop being so bloody human.

Gerard Manley Hopkins

G. HOPKINS, hopped, hoped by applying
Vaulting votivish verse verifying
    Alliterative Lit
    That's Liturgical it
Might preclude the daft dude deadly dying.

Hoped hapless HOP hopelessly. In
The circs moany MANLEY HOP's kin,
    After Jesu GED joins,
    Get him published! Then coins
From his royalties start rolling in!

For a gloomy life lived 'neath the aegis
Of the Society of Jesus*
    Meant, sans issue**, the swag
    In the Anglican bag
Of HOP's kin ended up! Well, hard cheeses.

* This rhyme's rime reaps rheums far as Lytham,
  For tis spunked from the trunk of sprung rhythm.

**To spell it out, all HOPKIN's issue
  Got soaked tween the folds of a tissue.

Emily Dickinson

As to poets who hid under rocks –
Miss EMILY DICKINSON's Frocks
    Were white – Short, her Verse –
    Her manners – quite terse –
With a ticked 'No Publicity' box...

The Aesthetic Movement

With more movements than most bowels, later
Oxford spawned, through WALTER PATER
    The Movement Aesthetic
    Which was just as pathetic
While stressing more than One Creator.

PATER preached Art For Art's Sake,
A basic commercial mistake
    Forcing down prices
    And fostering vices
That soon kept the horses awake.

Making matters worse, this Jeremiah
Proclaimed that 'All Art Doth Aspire
    To Music's Condition'
    A fact proved, cos Titian
Wrote sonnets in oil, in a choir.*

Did PATER care less? Did he heck!
He just stretched out his tortoise like neck
    And whispered 'I'm pallid
    But insist that it's valid
I prepare you for *le fin de siecle*!'

* Just try it yourself. For a starter
  Use a chisel to carve a cantata
  Then moving on get out your crayons
  For that symphony. It'll take aeons.

The Arts and Crafts Movement

Soon everyone, just through hard graft's
Improved by the Whole Arts & Crafts
    Movement! How pleasant
    The taste of the peasant!
Just ignore all those terrible draughts.

The Decadence

And at this point things get much steamier,
For Lit's now annexed by Bohemia
    And I don't mean the Czechs
    But those physical wrecks
Who'd look less shit suffering leukaemia.

They did it their way, like SINATRA,
Spreading Lit like a plague from Sumatra
    Though one has to doubt Frank
    Would choose garrets as dank
As the digs where they slummed in Montmartre.

The trailblazers were VERLAINE & RIMBAUD.
V fell at first sight for this glam beau
    Steeped in absinthe
    So placed Art on a plinth
Then stabbed him, still burning a flambeau*,

And both boys pissed out of his skull!
With these two around life's not dull –
    Which infers we would care
    For *UNE SAISON EN ENFER*
More than a whole lifetime in Hull!

* The Art in question? It's young RIMBAUD,
  Who nonetheless dodged that cold tombeau
  VERLAINE was planning for the bimbo
  As pink elephants straight out of Dumbo
  Had flung them both into some limbo
  Of drink madness, just like at Chrimbo;
  A Romantic, if quite deadly, combo.

VERLANE & RAMBO

Apology

(Forgive me. I don't wish to lumber
Those poets who live by the Humber
    With the idea they're boring
    Or unused to scoring
Opiates heralding slumber

Or suggest their behaviour's not scratchy
Or their personal hygiene not patchy.
    It's just that, pre-LARKIN,
    Few poets embark in
Dance routines like 'The Apache'

Or generally come on as crass
As the loafers and drunkards who pass
    As Poetry's Acme
    When they attack the
Passers-by in Montparnasse

And pretend that they're all acting cleverly
Or so artily you will never be
    As arty as them!
    If you want that (hem hem)
Kind of thing, best move to Beverley.)

The Yellow Book

VERLAINE and RIMBAUD, from France,
Thus ushered in The Decadence
    And those dark squalid groves
    Through which, in their droves,
Poets and writers now ponce.

Green carnations and deathly white lilies
Were clutched by boys down Piccadilly's
    Café Royal all night
    Though they all looked a fright
And gave each other the willies.

The shocked bourgeoisie could just look
In disgust as aesthetes undertook
    To refine their refinement
    Like a consumptive's confinement
To give birth to the... *YELLOW BOOK*!

Any daughter's mamma would've feared she
Might read the thing and go quite weird! See?
    The girl's next appeared
    As a fey aesthete's beard
All thanks to the drawings of BEARDSLEY!

Yet these aesthetes' ev'ry urbane quip meant
The *YELLOW BOOK* sent a fresh shipment
    Of Art to the Ages
    (Though try *YELLOW PAGES*
When you want to hire disco equipment).

Oscar

But Aestheticism's élan
Before long got washed down the pan.
     When OSCAR got cozy
     With horrid young BOSEY
The Shit hit *LADY WINDERMERE'S FAN*.

When faced with QUEENSBURY's bile,
It was proven at OSCAR WILDE's trial
     Though to be EARNEST oughtn't
     Be judged less important
Than the power of Wit to Beguile,

Where Love dare not yet speak its name,
When WILDE plays QUEENSBURY's game*
     OSCAR's daredevilry'll
     Mean a queen's burial
And Queensburys win, to our shame.

Poor OSCAR was sentenced to goal
In Reading, which didn't entail
     Much reading. This sunders
     (With *DE PROFUNDIS*)
The BOSEY pash, which had grown stale.

As he left gaol he thought 'Might I still
Be remembered although, fat and ill,
     I'll die soon in Paris?'
     And maybe FRANK HARRIS
Replied 'You will, OSCAR, you will!'

* THE MARQUIS OF QUEENSBURY drools
  But you play at his games by his rules.

OSCAR WILDE
VS. JACK THE RIPPER

The City of Dreadful Night

OSCAR's fate's hardly vanilla,
Crushed 'tween CHARYBDIS & SCILLA*
    But we mustn't forget
    The considerable debt
Owed him by th'Victorian Thriller...

In *THE PICTURE OF DORIAN GRAY*
A beautiful chap goes astray
    And has chicks by the bedful!**
    It's no penny dreadful
Though it plays in a similar way

With themes in more popular fiction
With its schizophrenic depiction
    Of double lives, lies
    And where somebody dies
In a dark urban den of affliction!

Through that *CITY OF DREADFUL NIGHT*,
Of fogbound streets pocked by gaslight
    Prowled DORIAN, who spied
    Both JEKYLL and HYDE!
But which one would win in a fight?

And if we then widen the bout
Would DRACULA bite the throat out –
    Once he got snarly –
    Of, say, SVENGALI
Who mesmerised TRILBY, the lout!

* Hypocrisy leavened with spite
  Had rolled poor old OSC in the shite.

** His youthful looks fooled them. How soft!
  They'd not seen what was up in his loft...

Up the Empire

If all of them fought JACK THE RIPPER
Would each end up sliced like a kipper,
    Even the vempire?*
    Thank God the Empire
Was there to make people feel chipper!

For although your poverty's crippling
And your muscles are wasted, not rippling
    If you fought for the QUEEN
    You might end up seen
In some Poetry written by KIPLING!!

* If this spelling seems quite contrarian
  Remember the vamp was Hungarian
  (Although, as we know, Transylvania
  Was later annexed by Romania).

Barrack Room Ballads

Gor blimey and stone the crows, mush!
As we 'eads orf for that 'Indoo Kush
 It's 'Tommy! You're thick
 So die fer Queen Vic!'
I s'pose that's orl right at a push.

If –

If you can keep your head while those
Around all lose theirs, then this shows
    If you can keep cool
    And not play the fool
You might end up a Man, I suppose.

Recessional

The tumult and the shouting dies.
Kings and Captains depart. No surprise.
    Lord, be with us yet
    In case we forget
When we get cut down to size

(The rest of KIPLING, by and large,
Was bigging it up viz The Raj
    Although in World War One
    It was no longer fun
Thanks to the idiots in charge).

But in verse on Imperialist War
KIPLING, when we fought the Boer
    Was pushed out of the way! We
    Got HOUSMAN, AE,
Who wrote about Shropshire amour.

A Shropshire Lad

In Shropshire there once was this lad
Who was laddish and wild and quite bad*
    And dead at one-and-twenty
    Exactly like plenty
Of others. How terribly sad.

* I think we'll gloss over the thrills
  To be had by blue remembered hills....

The Late Victorian Novel

In the late Victorian era
It really could not have been clearer
    That on top of aesthetes,
    The Empire & grease-sheets*
The Novel gushed forth like Old Thera!**

Moreover it transformed Eng Lit
And made everyone proud as a Brit!
    This was done, on the whole,
    By a Yank and a Pole
Which should not surprise us one bit.

*   Slang for books of that common unrare sort
    That these days you buy in an airport.

** The volcano that History's shown
    Totally fucked the Minoan.

Henry James

So everyone rightly acclaims
Novels penned by HENRY JAMES
 Of Yanks oh so gauche
 That when they act posh
They put off their rich Old World flames,

Which facts stylistically JAMES aims
To describe in the way that he frames
 Sub-adverbial clauses
 Showing Louis Quatorze's
Furniture not unproclaims

How her not un-outloud wild claims
That he not unwholly played games
 Across sentences wending
 Through paras unending...
By which time you've forgotten their names.

None of which detracts from all the fame's
JAMES's due though, with the dames
 What *MASIE KNEW*
 Was *A TURN OF THE SCREW*
Was unlikely from old HENRY JAMES.

(At this point I'd now hoped to precis
All HENRY JAMES' novels. How spacey
 We'd feel at the rush
 Of this haute-bourgeois slush,
It is so incredibly racy!

But instead just try *living* his oeuvre!
Be rich and/or poor [in French; *pauvre*]
 Try both Innocence and Guilt!
 Sew a New England Quilt
In Paris! I think that should serve....)

Joseph Conrad

The novels of KORZENIOWSKI
Made English Lit's many toffs plea:
    'Though they tell of the briny
    And are bright, new and shiny,
Sell these novels at one penny off! See,

Under his *nom de plume*, JOSEPH CONRAD,
He writes books about chaps who have gone bad;
    And woes maritime!
    Plans which miscarry chime
With the readers, we know. It's beyond sad

Then that Eng. isn't JOE's Mother Tongue!
Tales of far-flung lands should stay unsung!
    It's too unbecoming!
    Let Poles stick to plumbing!
For such presumptions men have hung!'

This racism seemed inauspicious,
So the ironies then proved delicious
    When, though controversial
    It turned out commercial
To write *NIGGER OF THE NARCISSUS*!*

* The n-word back then had less heft.
  It's a world that I'm thankful we've left.

Heart of Darkness

An ivory trader called KURTZ,
So caught up in his work that it hurts,
    Shows that things can wrong, oh
    So far up The Congo
It burdens the global *Weltschmertz*!

MARLOW, a sailor, narrates
How ruthlessly pursuing freight's
    Infected KURTZ fungally.
    The bugger's gone jungly!
(Though at very competitive rates)

Months of steaming upstream, what's M find?
That KURTZ has gone out of his mind.
    Steaming downstream, in bed,
    'MISTAH KURTZ' – Shit! – 'He dead'
Let misery be unconfined!

You see, with colonial trade
We all should be very afraid.
    The Horror! The Horror!
    Will come up tomorror!
While dark places will stay in the shade.*

* And if it's dark places you seek
  Forget Africa! Try Deptford Creek...

AN IVORY MERCHANT...

That life's a bitch then you die
Is clearly the main reason why
    This book, let's admit,
    Has obsessed Eng Lit Crit,
Though the Africans' plight's by the bye.

KURTZ's hubris and fate merely show it's
Existentially horrid. We know it's
    To point out the angst
    Which is common amangst
Any number of top Western poets**

** I don't think that I have to spelliot
   Out, but I mean TS Eliot...

Lord Jim

JIM was a sailor, and JIM's
Jumped ship! Abandoning pilgrims
    Embarked on the haj
    Tends, by and large,
To reflect rather badly on him.

The Board of Inquiry looked grim;
After judgement JIM's prospects looked dim...
    By the way, did I mention
    The theme is Redemption
In this CONRAD book titled *LORD JIM*?

Disgraced, he goes out on a limb,
Gets a job on the Pacific Rim
    Where he's called 'Tuan' or 'Lord'
    So his self-respect soared
And he no longer felt a vic-tim!

Up turns a notorious crim
And despite reassurance from JIM
    Kills the chief's son. Redemption
    Finds JIM, by extension,
When the chief shoots him dead! Well, get him.

The Secret Agent

A purveyor of porn name of VERLOC
Spied for all sides – no shit, Sherlock!
 Til the treacherous creep
 Had got in so deep
To escape he'd be needing an airlock.

VERLOC's wife WINNIE concedes
That Propaganda by the Deed's
 OK, but she's rather
 VERLOC be a father
To her bro STEVIE, who's special needs.

V's control states: 'Create a furore!
Blow up Greenwich Observatory
 To discredit the Red!'
 STEVIE's blown up instead
And surrounding trees covered in glory.

The Heat's on! (HEAT's the Special Branch cop).
Is the Mad Bomber PROF* for the drop?
 HEAT tells WINNIE 'bout STEVIE;
 She doesn't just grieve, she
Makes sure VERLOC now gets the chop!

WINNIE flees for France, where the bureaux are
With OSSIPON*, who ne'er o'erthrew a Tsar.
    He runs off with her cash;
    WINNIE drowns with a splash.
This wouldn't have happened on Eurostar...

* The PROF's tooled to blow up so then
  Others die. He's a virus 'midst men,
  While OSSIPON's red politics
  Are paid for by him turning tricks,
  Unlike MICHAELIS, whose theories
  Are subsidised by high-class dearies.
  And CONRAD depicts this whole catchment
  With a studied ironic detatchment.

Nostromo

In Costaguana* NOSTROMO**
Serves as the brave major-domo
    Of the local elite
    Who are facing defeat
By the rebels! The 'Whisky a-Go-Go'

Lures some tars but not good NOSTROMO!
He smuggles out silver in slo-mo
    With DECOUD, a hack,
    While under attack
From rebels like JOSHUA NKOMO.***

Silver's beached on an isle! Stout NOSTROMO
Swims home, leaving DECAUD. Qui bono?
    Not DECAUD: goes loco,
    Tops himself! How rococo.
But NOSTROMO's now hardly a promo

For lack of corruption! NOSTROMO
Starts nicking the silver! A no-no!
    And Life proves much cheaper:
    The old lighthouse keeper
Shoots NOSTROMO dead. *Ecce Homo*!

*   The Costaguana, I have heard
    Depends on the shit of each bird...

** NOSTROMO's real name's JOE FIDANZA,
    And that is the end of this stanza.

*** Other rebels, eg R MUGABE
    Might be cited here, although far be
    It from me to say that I'd rather
    Cite someone like CHE GUEVARA.

Under Western Eyes

The student RASUMOV shopped HALDIN
The Assassin, but then he got called in
    By the cops! He must spy
    On exiles! Live a lie!
No wonder the bugger feels walled in.

The exiles find out he's a sham
When he 'fesses it's all been am-dram,
    So them render him deaf!
    Strike me pink! What the eff?
And then he's knocked down by a tram!

Victory

From the island of Samburon HEYST,
A man with whom Fortune had diced,
    Went to Sourabaya
    Where SCHOMBERG, a liar
And hotelier planned to get spliced

To LENA, from the All-Girl Band.
But things didn't go as he'd planned:
    It was HEYST left with LENA!
    Deus ex Machina
From SCHOMBERG then gets out of hand.

Led by MR JONES, misogynist,
Some thugs came to break up their tryst
    (JONES was the campest).
    As it's based on *THE TEMPEST**
You've probably now got the gyst.

JONES' gang all get killed (JONES is drowned),
LENA's wounded and dies, and that sound,
    With no prospect of wife,
    After HEYST takes his life,
Is his house burning down to the ground!

* If you don't like this couplet, please mock me,
  Then say it in Belgravia Cockney.

Intermission

Move forward to 1915.
You've read *VICTORY* on a latrine
    In a dank frontline trench
    Which is filled with the stench
Of mud, blood, shit, piss and phosgene.

Still, although this might strike you as tardy
As you scratch at the lice 'neath your cardy
    And couldn't feel wearier,
    Let's try something cheerier
Than CONRAD. I know! THOMAS HARDY

Is what's required! *Oubliez la guerre*
And breathe in that rank country air:
    The stink of the soil
    And the backbreaking toil
And that lovely dark rural despair!

Far from the Madding Crowd

'Though BATHSHEBA,' sighed GABRIEL OAK,
'Is badly in need of a poke,
　　Since my sheepdog – sniff sniff –
　　Fucked moi flock o'er a cliff
She thinks Oi'm a bit of a joke.'

Then the shepherd helps put out a fire
On a farm – owned by his heart's desire!
　　He's hired! Oh good!
　　Then WILLIAM BOLDWOOD
Proposes. BATH tells GABE, 'Retire!'

But when all BATH's sheep get the bloat's
GABE who cures all. A redcoat's
　　Turned up. SERGEANT TROY!
　　Who would also annoy
BOLDWOOD once he's getting his oats

From BATHSHEBA! But TROY still loves FANNY,
His ex-bride found starved in a cranny
　　Who dies! Next TROY drowns
　　And BOLDWOOD unfrowns,
Pursues BATH, but TROY'S back! It's uncanny!

To conclude, BOLDWOOD now shoots dead TROY.
Doesn't hang as he's mad (it's a ploy).
　　But this still means GABE OAK
　　Can essay a poke
With BATHSHEBA at last! Boy oh boy!

The Return of the Native

The Native Returning is CLYM,
A Parisian jeweller (get him!),
    Returned in the belief
    That round Egdon Heath
They need schoolmasters cos they're all dim.

CLYM marries EUSTACIA VYE,
Who'd once caught Innkeep WILDEVE's eye.
    She's in the belief
    That she'll soon leave the Heath
With CLYM, who goes blind. And you'd cry

If that was the end. It gets worse*
CLYM's now re-duced to cutting furze*!
    It gets even madder:
    CLYM's mum's bit by an adder
And WILDEVE now seeks to coerce*

EUSTACIA to sin! In his grief
CLYM blames EUST for mum's death. The chief
    Parties, I fear,
    All now fall in a weir
And two are soon buried beneath

Egdon Heath! Thankfully, CLYM's not dead
And soon takes up preaching instead.
    WILDEVE's widow then
    Weds DIGGORY VENN
The Reddleman, who's very red!

---

* If you doubt these rhymes work, I aver
  That they do in the thick Wessex burr...

Tess of the d'Urbervilles

JOHN DURBEYFIELD'S white trash, I'd guess,
But is told by the PARSON, 'Why, yes!
    You're of D'URBERVILLE stock!
    You're noble!' It's cock.
At the May Day dance JOHN's daughter TESS

Sees ANGEL CLARE, who doth impress.
Then as dad's drunk TESS, under duress,
    Goes to market. Of course
    She kills their one horse!
Calls on D'URBERVILLES* to ease her stress.

Meets ALEC, a lech. Intumesce
Does this cad soon as he sees young TESS
    Then rapes her (well, maybe)**
    TESS then has a baby
Called SORROW who dies. *Quelle tristesse*!

Now a milkmaid TESS can reassess
Her chances with ANGEL. Success!
    His prim pious folks
    Like her good breeding! Jokes!
Wedding night: she decides to confess...

* These D'URBERVILLES are nouveau riche
   Parvenus. Ain't life a biche?

** The scene is ambiguously written
   To avoid shocking prudes ruling Britain...

Though he's screwed around too forgiveness
Don't inform ANGEL's uxoriousness.
    He leaves for Brazil
    Where he gets very ill.
TESS meets AL – now a preacherman! Bless!

AL still leches for TESS nonetheless
And they set up as cad and mistress.
    Then ANGEL returns,
    Begs forgiveness; TESS spurns
ANGEL, sees AL... well, just guess

What's likely to happen next. Yes!
ALEC's murdered by TESS! What a mess!
    TESS AND ANGEL arrenge
    A tryst in Stone Henge.
Then she's subject to Law's due process

And hanged as a foul murderess.
If this ending's inclined to depress
    It ain't much of a riddle,
    Just a sweet rural idyll,
And that's HARDY's oeuvre, more or less!

WOSSAT BABES? THA KIDDIES'VE AWL 'UNG 'EMSELVES AN NAH YOU GONNA SELL ME DAHN THE FAIR? WOT A LARF EH?

BIBLE

THE ONLY WAY IS WESSEX

The Mayor of Casterbridge

HENCHARD sells to a tar at the fair
Wife and daughter, 5 guineas the pair,
    To recharge his flagon!
    Then goes on the wagon
To CASTERBRIDGE, to become Mayor!

Years pass. Wife and daughter repair
To Casterbridge. H dare not share
    Their previous fate
    With the electorate;
Dumps fiancée to wed old wife. There

Can be no harm in that! FARFRAE* shares
Laissez-faire skills to run the affairs
    Of H, whose wife dies!
    Then he gets a surprise:
That daughter's not his! So he scares

Her to the ex-fiancée's lair.
Ex-f's married FARFRAE, but there
    Are some old love letters
    Made public! Upset, her's
Soon dead of a fit! And the Mayor?

He's broke and in friendless despair!
Daughter's real dad's back! Time for a hair
    Of the dog, I should say,
    Once the girl's wed FARFRAE.
Then H dies on the heath. That seems fair.

* Though this character should, I confess,
  Be in *FARFRAE THE MADDING CROWD*, yes?

Jude the Obscure

You'd imagine that JUDE THE OBSCURE'd
Become to misfortune inured:
    His missus is crude;
    His cuz, SUE, a prude;
And his scholarship caricatured.

Nonetheless JUDE doth conclude
Relations with both, which is rude.
    His boss tells him 'You're
    Dismissed! You're impure!'
But he's now got an increasing brood!

Things are hard. Eldest kid spots a cure.
'It's the high cost of each plat du jour!
    We children intrude:
    If we die there's more food;
We are too menny. Now we're fewer!'

Kids hang. Sue gets God. JUDE gets stewed
And entrapped by his wife again! Dude!
    Then dies with the allure
    Of thick Wessex manure.
My, what verisimilitude!*

* Navel gazing at life in a hovel,
  JUDE was T HARDY'S last novel.

The Fabians

If you think HARDY's view of the Present
Refracted through Time is unpleasant
    Why not try the Future?
    More likely to suit ya
Is Justice for Worker and Peasant!

It's Class that's at fault. Any baby can
See that, and therefore see maybe an
    Alternative! Crush
    The Boss! But don't rush,
For that's not the path of the Fabian.

The Fabians were led by the WEBBS,
And moved sideways, slowly, like crebs*.
    Red, vegetarian,
    Valetudinarian**
They boast several Eng Lit Celebs!

* If this rhyme so contrived gets you down,
   It's the sound of the smart part of town.

** Although weedy, sexual scandals
   Defined them, like open-toed sandals.

George Bernard Shaw

To name but three, GEORGE BERNARD SHAW
Wrote comedies we all adore
    Like... er... *MY FAIR LADY*
    And he liked stuff quite shady
Like Nietzsche and Stalin. What's more

He thought spelling in English was muck.
Wrote an alphabet. Lor luvva duck!
    This was far less misleading
    To people when reading
It. 𐑖 𐑒 𐑦 𐑕 𐑞 𐑝 𐑕 𐑦 𐑕 𐑕 𐑕 𐑡𐑑𐑔?!

Shaw also wrote *MAN AND SUPERMAN*.
The musical, score based on Couperin*,
    Bombed in Des Moines
    And so didn't join
The American Songbook. A trooper an'

A Socialist Shaw shrugged and said
'Box Office don't bother a red,
    Nor my place in the charts!
    I'll stick with the Arts
And knock off a Preface instead!'

* With lyrics and book by L HART
  DON JUAN IN HELL at the start
  Of the second act sadly appeared to
  Revolt everyone in the theatre...

HG Wells

More futurish was HG WELLS
Whose notorious eye for the gels
    Meant among *THINGS TO COME*
    After he had were some
Kids from each mademoiselle.

More Uplifting is Travel through Time
To futurity's new paradigm,
    Though Morlocks and Elois
    Show that boys will be boys
Forever, like Capitalist crime.

Then, with *THE FIRST MEN ON THE MOON*
And *WAR IN THE AIR* he'd attune
    Us to what we'd see next
    (Though that seminal text
THE INVISIBLE MAN is immune).

He also wrote History, provoking
Dispute, and some novels invoking
    The Petty Bourgeois
    A lot of whom are
Homeowners in or near Woking.*

* Where life is good until WELLS harshens
  Things; that's where he lands his Martians.

A Fabian Confusion

Before leaving the Fabians we gotta
Correct what might seems as a blot, a
    Black mark writ beside
    SYD WEBB's*choice as his bride:
She was BEATRICE and not BEATRIX Potter.

But how can you tell them apart?
Cos BEATRICE & BEATRIX both chart
    A Society which fails,
    In hideous tales
That pierce everyone to the heart.

Each one of these dame's output features
The plight of poor downtrodden creatures,
    Though making them edible
    Makes BEATRIX more credible,
With the breadth her propaganda reaches!

* To confuse things yet further there's two
  Of these WEBBS, SYD AND PHILIP. Who knew?
  PHIL's a partner in Morris & Co
  With WILLIAM. SYD's Fabian, so
  While with SYD it's current affairs
  With PHILIP, well, mostly it's chairs.

The Edwardians

We now reach a period of flux
Before Modernism wholly fucks*
    The whole of Eng Lit!
    But who gives a shit?*
First here's some Edwardian schmucks...

(You needn't despair, wet the bed
Or feel like a fool if instead
    Of familiarity
    You feel a disparity
With this lot: they're now all unread...)

* If you reckon this language obscene
  It's simply to show what I mean...

Chelloc and Besterton

GK CHESTERTON and HILAIRE BELLOC
Were both venerating a relloc*
    When, beyond hope,
    They spotted the Pope
And both of them tugged at their fe'lock.

CHESTERTON gained his renown
By badmouthing Jews about town
    In ways that could frighten.
    Then off he went writin'
'Bout the Vatican dick, FATHER BROWN.

BELLOC, meanwhile, would apportion
To Jews every crime from abortion
    To usury and worse.
    Still, he wrote funny verse
For kiddiwinks. My, what a Caution!

So small-minded they're Lilliputian,
Such attitudes stink like pollution
    But if you're R.C.
    That's the thing, don't you see?
Say sorry – you get Absolution!

* This relic displayed 'neath the rood?
  The Holy Arse Bone of St Jude!

Arnold Bennett

It is an unquestionable tenet
That Prosperity's not for you when it
    Turns out Life's Lottery's
    Seen you born in the Potteries.
Unless, of course, you're ARNOLD BENNETT.

The Novels of EM Forster

In *A ROOM WITH A VIEW*, EM FORSTER
Implies LUCY resorts to Morse ter
    Communicate brittly
    Til GEORGE, thanks to Italy,
Surplanted VYSE and intercoursed her!

In *A PASSAGE TO INDIA*, FORSTER
Revealed DR AZIZ had crorsed a
    Line in a cave –
    Or not – but forgave
ADELA. The Raj, though, endorsed her!

In *HOWARD'S END*, writes EM FORSTER,
Unfeeling rich snobs reinforced a
    System which wrecked
    Everything! Just connect
Even if your son's banged up in borster[l]!*

* In other words, trust your vocation,
  Location Location Location!

... Some MERCHANT IVORY...

...AN IVORY MERCHANT & SOME
MERCHANT IVORY!

John Galsworthy

GALSWORTHY, J. did of course write
THE FORSYTE SAGA in which bores fight.
    Now eight decades dead
    Galsworthy's unread
Which he could've worked out with some foresight.*

* One supposes that that Nobel Prize
  Failed to make the scales fall from his eyes...

The Wind in the Willows

When the Pastorally Mawkish* applies ter
The Thing, and a poor weasel tries ter
   Get the justice he's owed
   From a rich, reckless toad
Who wins? The amphibious shyster!

* Dawn's Gate's Piper seldom doth tarry,
   But this mole**... Is this stuff by LE CARRÉ?

** Ratted on by a badger! Is that
   Less worse than badgered by a rat?

Peter Pan

From his repressed Id BARRIE span
This pervy play. Could this boy/man
    Maintain a boner?
    'Floreat Etona!'
Cries HOOK when he's murdered by PAN!

Beatrix Potter

Nature's red in tooth and claw. Pick
Your species and you're still dumb, poor, thick
    And condemned to be brutal
    Except when you're cute! All
'S redeemed once you're anthropomorphic.

But with POTTER it's quite the reverse.
Her creatures live under the curse
    Of always aspiring
    To be us, and it's tiring
Putting clothes on – though often it's worse.

You're a brute, after all. Life is fleetin'
And your family's already meat 'n'
    2 veg! For it's written
    If pig, mouse or kitten
The likelihood is you'll be eaten.

It's even worse if you're a bunny:
MACGREGOR's plans for you aren't funny.
    So it's doubly unjust
    That the National Trust
Has entwee'd your plight just to make money!!*

* On exiting don't fail to stop
  To buy merchandise in our Gift Shop.

The Celtic Twilight

While Edwardian authors got squiffy
In Ireland things became iffy
    When artists cried 'Why fight
    In this Celtic Twilight
By these banks of the sundappled Liffey?

From Moher which is oh so cliffy
Cross the Bogs which themselves are quite whiffy,
    It is our opeenion
    You should not get Fenian
When Folk Lore not Land War's more pithy!'

Young YEATS at this point got quite sniffy
Steeped in the ways of Theosiffy,*
    Art's *sine qua non*!
    Then he thought of MAUDE GONNE.
LADY GREGORY blushed at Yeats' stiffy!**

* The Order of the Golden Dawn
   Meant that YEATS didn't really need porn.

** But once LADY G became gabby
   YEATS wisely steered clear of The Abbey.

The Lake Isle of Innisfree

I will arise and go now
Not to Dundee or Macau
    But to Innisfree
    Where I'll live with a bee
And some peace I'll be having there. Ciao!

The Second Coming

The falcon's deaf; things fall apart
And the centre won't hold but impart
    Mere anarchy loose!
    The best are obtuse
While the worst of them? Don't make me start!

Second Coming's coming! What spawn
Of lion and man, with a yawn,
    After ages of grouches
    Sullenly slouches
Towards Bethlehem to be born?

The Georgians

While the Irish were off busy forgin'
A national aesthetic engorgin'
    The whole bloody thing
    From YEATS to J SYNGE,
The English moved on to be GEORGIAN...*

* J SYNGE sounds a bit like Jay Z
  Who's a rapper, though neither could be
  Reckoned as quiet
  As one caused a riot
  With *PLAYBOY OF THE WESTERN WORLD*. See?

Katherine Mansfield

'I'm ill,' she sobbed. MIDDLETON MURRAY
Told KATHERINE MANSFIELD, 'Don't worry!
   When your lips are so soft...'
   Then the poor woman coughed
And they said to each other 'Let's hurry!'

DH Lawrence

But decent folk viewed with abhorrence
The Life and Work of DH LAWRENCE*
    Who dreamed about MILFs**
    And whose written down filth's
Likely to summon forth warrants!***

Yet though the rich rain fell in torrents
On the thick mucky mud, DH LAWRENCE
    Left home one dark morn
    When they said he wrote porn
With its various cultural cross-corrents****

Which he wove into prose wild and fervant!
Here's a word to the wise and observant:
    Do not read the oeuvre
    Of this Nietzschean perve,
And don't let your wife or your servant!*****

---

*   NB. Here's DH, not TE,
       Who's DOA. DH? TB.
       Between Sex and Death it's being dead you win.
       DH liked bed; TE, Bedouin.

**   But who did he dream of, dear reader?
       His own mum, or was it of FRIEDA?

***   I mean warrants for his arrest
       For getting some stuff off his chest.

**** In Notts this ere rhyme's in good order,
       And in Mehico, South of the Border!

***** This filth's not obscene though. I foggart
       This was proved by the late Richard Hoggart.

Ford Madox Ford

Want a novelist you can afford?
Then why not try FORD MADOX FORD
    Who'd been FORD MADOX HUEFFER
    Which means you get two for
The price of one, plus a reward!

The reward was FORD's many Reviews
Which he edited, full of adieus
    To The Old. That's the cue
    For the birth of The New
And that's how FORD made THE NEW news!

The Stock of The New therefore soared
As experience of Newnessness scored
    Which is why they'd've told ya
    When he wrote *THE GOOD SOLDIER*
He was known as 'Modal(i)ty Ford'!*

But why then did FORD change his name?
Here we get to the name of the game.
    For, to thunderous applause
    The War To End Wars
Breaks out! Things would not be the same.

* 'Modal(i)ty': 'Model T'. Geddit?
  Plus he wrote *PARADE'S END*. Have you read it?

The Origins of the Great War

The Great War has always been spun
As generally being begun
    By a far archduke's heave-ho
    In Sarajevo*
And the marked beastliness of The Hun.

But like Trouble wrapped in bags of kit
This simplifies things just a bit
    For the genuine cause
    Of The War to End Wars
Is firmly embedded in Lit.

The source of this great cataclysm?
That you needed to think up an -ism
    If you sought The Profound –
    Plus a mad, sweaty POUND
And everything's dripping in gism!

Imagism, that is. Then with *BLAST*
The Vorticists blew up The Past
    Until all were sodden
    In blood – but that's Modern!
And the Futurists went very fast.

Imagism

Eg. 'The red wheelbarrow now
Stands by the sty. A pink sow
　　Oinks. And again
　　The dog stands in the rain
Petals on a wet, black bow-wow.'

The War

That's one side, all Modern and Hot,
But what about that other lot
    Bathed in the benison
    Of ALFRED, LORD TENNYSON
And weighed down by metre and plot?

As traditionalists these dumb mensches
Were slaughtered like pigs in the trenches
    While ELIOT and POUND
    Were swanning around
London salons. Oh how the gut wrenches!

But who wins? The young chap a Colonel
Sends over the top to eternal
    Resting hereafter
    Or he who cruel laughter
Brings forth with his latest Lit journal?

Either way, it would be an omission
To write off young writers patrician
    Many who, to be blunt,
    Hated things up the Front*
But still fulfilled war's grave commission**

*   Though I should perhaps let this point pass
    'Up the Front' here means not up the arse.

** In the War GRAVES ne'er saw stuff as gaudy as
    What happens each page in *I CLAUDIUS*.

Rupert Brooke

If I should die think this of me
In a foreign field's corner you'll see
    Some England, plus dust,
    And you also might just
See there's still honey for tea.*

* Is this fair? Poor sod died! Though, if warier,
  I suspect he'd have still got malaria...

Wilfred Owen

My subject is War and War's pity.
For War is a bore, and it's shitty.
    And here comes a battle!
    We'll all die like cattle.
But nonetheless try out this ditty:

Dulce et decorum est
Pro Patria mori. You've guessed.
    They're cunts. We're all goners.
    This war without honour's
Tbh left me quite unimpressed.*

* In fact I would howl at the moon,
  Though I'll leave that to SIEGFRIED SASSOON...

THEY DIED
SO MRS DALLOWAY
MAY BE
PUBLISHED